AMERICAN PANORAMA
Arranged by EUGÉNIE ROCHEROLLE
A Selection of Patriotic and Folk Tunes

CONTENTS

Editor: James L. King III
Art Layout: Valentin Miloje
Production Coordinator: Maudlyn Cooley

IT'S A GRAND OL' FLAG

Arranged by EUGÉNIE R. ROCHEROLLE

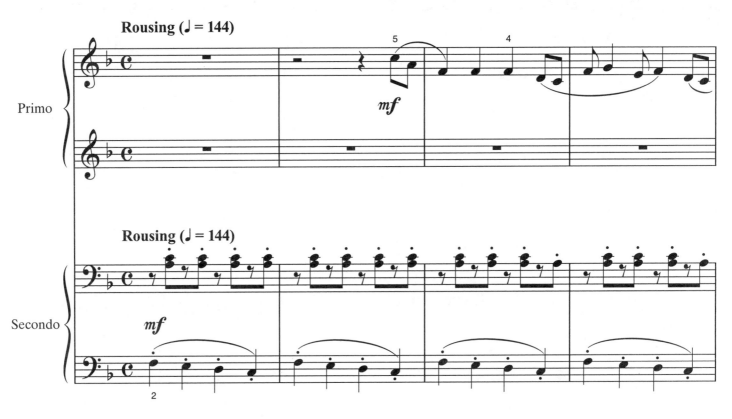

7

PAM0501

STAR-SPANGLED PRELUDE

Arranged by EUGÉNIE R. ROCHEROLLE

PAM0501

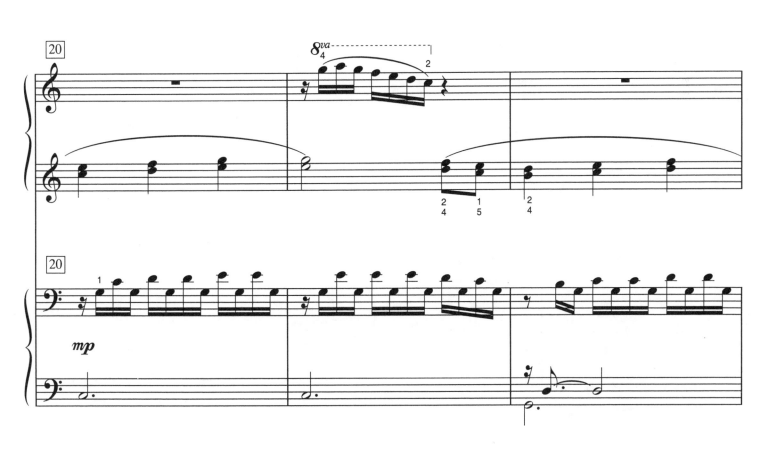

12

PAM0501

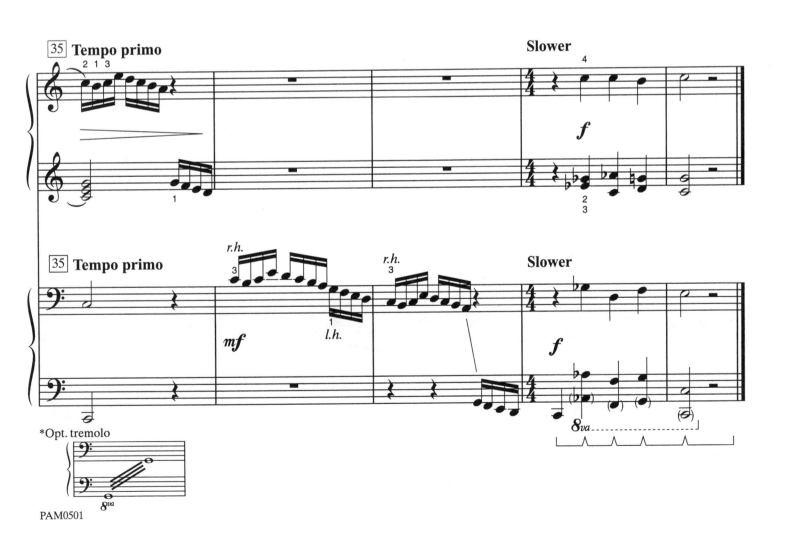

*Opt. tremolo

PAM0501

SHENANDOAH

Arranged by *EUGÉNIE R. ROCHEROLLE*

16

PAM0501

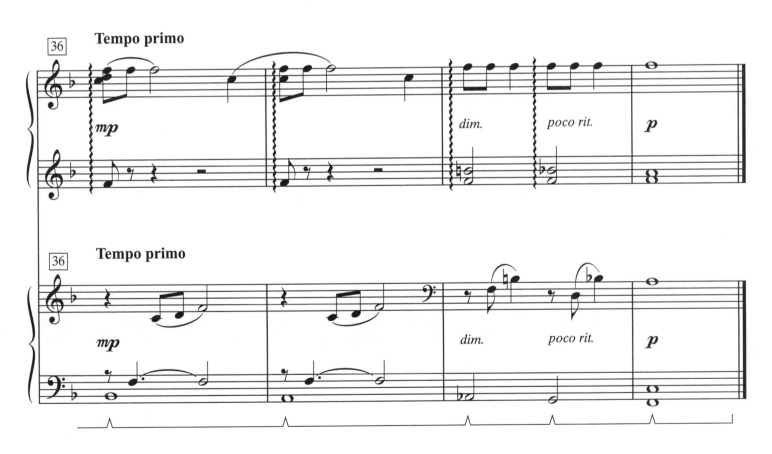

commissioned by Sheila Powers Converse

VARIATIONS ON RED RIVER VALLEY

Arranged by EUGÉNIE R. ROCHEROLLE

Variation I
Moderato (♩ = 112)

Moderato (♩ = 112)

22

PAM0501

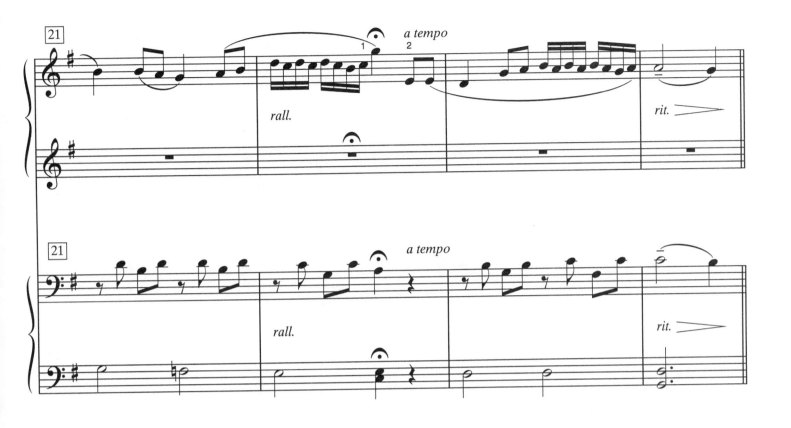

Variation II Molto allegro (♩. = 88)

Variation III
Larghetto (♩ = 60-66)

simile

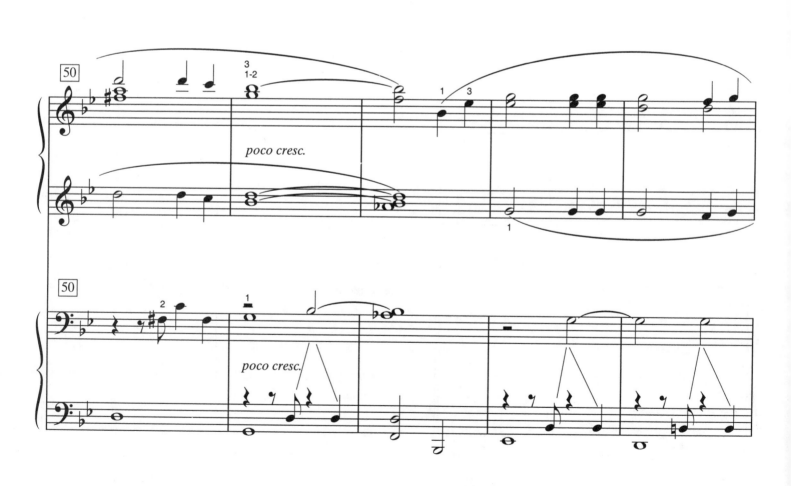

poco cresc.

poco cresc.

Variation IV
Allegro (♩ = 132)

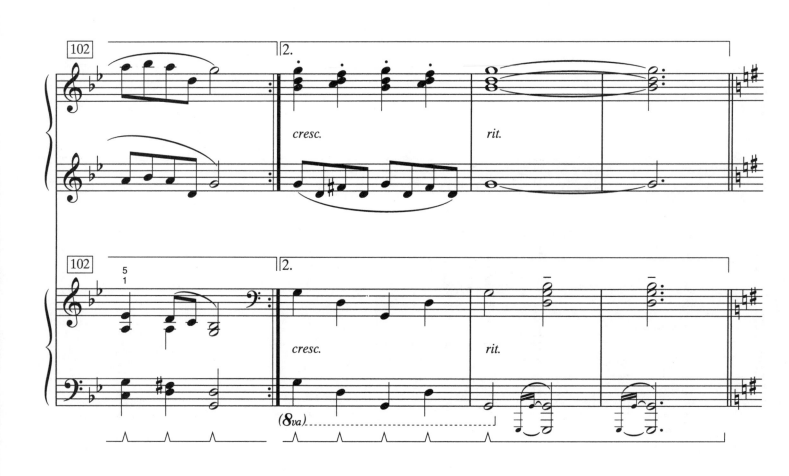

Variation V
Allegro (♩ = 138)

Allegro (♩ = 138)

EUGÉNIE ROCHEROLLE

Eugénie Rocherolle, composer, lyricist, pianist, and teacher, began an early publishing career in choral music and in 1978, with the success of her first piano solo collection, established herself as one of the leading American composers of piano repertoire.

A graduate from Newcomb College of Tulane University, Eugénie also had a course of study with Nadia Boulanger in Paris. In 1995 she was honored as the outstanding Newcomb alumna. A "Commissioned by Clavier" composer, she was also one of seven composer members of the National League of American Pen Women whose works were chosen to be presented in a concert at the Terrace Theater in the Kennedy Center. Awards from the Pen Women include a first place for both piano and choral in biennial national competitions. Among her commissions are works for combined chorus and orchestra and for solo and duo piano.

Mrs. Rocherolle's creative output also includes works for solo voice, chorus, concert band, musical theater, and chamber music. Her piano publications include original music for the *WB Solo Library* and the *Composer Spotlight Series,* arrangements for the *WB Christian Piano Library* and *Looney Tunes Piano Library,* as well as independent works for solo piano; one piano, four hands; and two pianos. She is a member of the American Society of Composers, Authors and Publishers (ASCAP); Connecticut Composers Inc.; and the National Federation of Music Clubs. Her biographical profile appears in the *International Who's Who in Music, Baker's Biographical Dictionary of 20th Century Classical Musicians, International Encyclopedia of Women Composers, Who's Who of American Women,* and *Who's Who in the East.*

Mrs. Rocherolle currently maintains a private studio in Connecticut where she teaches piano and composition.